WHY BIRDS
DO THAT

Why Birds Do That

40 Distinctive Bird Behaviors Explained & Photographed

Text by Michael Furtman
Photographs by Steve & Dave Maslowski

Willow Creek Press

Published by Willow Creek Press
P.O. Box 147, Minocqua, Wisconsin 54548

Editor/Design: Andrea K. Donner

Library of Congress Cataloging-in-Publication Data .
Furtman, Michael.
  Why birds do that : 40 distinctive bird behaviors explained & photographed / Michael Furtman.
     p. cm.
   ISBN 1-59543-059-8 (hardcover : alk. paper)
  1. Birds--Behavior. I. Title.
QL698.3.F98 2004
598.15--dc22

                                        2004012993

Printed in the United States of America

Table of Contents

Why do birds stand on one leg? 9

Why aren't birds electrocuted when they sit on wires? 11

Why do birds sing, and why mostly in the morning? 13

Why do some birds fly as a flock? 17

Why do some chicks hatch naked, and others hatch covered with down? . .19

Why do some birds have multiple broods per year? 23

Why do birds bathe? 25

Why do birds molt? 27

Why do birds of the same species often look different
  in the spring than in the fall or winter? 29

Why do bird beaks come in so many shapes and sizes? 31

Why do birds preen? 33

Why do birds establish territories? 35

Why do male birds have brighter colors than females? 37

Why do birds migrate? 39

Why do some birds have short, broad wings, and others
    have long, tapered wings?.. 41

Why do birds seem to eat constantly? 43

Why do male birds "strut their stuff" during mating season? 45

Why do eggs hatch all at the same time, even when laid days apart?...... 47

Why do some birds "dump" their eggs in the nests of
    other birds, even birds of other species? 49

Why do birds seem to know their way during migration? 51

Why do some birds nest in trees, while others nest on the ground? 53

Why do some birds live solitary lives, while others flock together? 55

Why do males of some species stay with the female and
    their young, while in other species, the male departs?................ 57

Why do some birds mate for life? 59

Why do the feet of birds not freeze in extreme cold?.................. 61

Why do some birds hunker down when an avian predator
    flies overhead, while others erupt into flight? 63

Why do birds of different species sometimes flock and feed together? 65

Why do some birds hunt at night, and others in the day? 67

Why do ground-feeding birds, like the American Robin, cock
    their heads to the side?... 69

Why do crows move into human neighborhoods, and why do
   some songbird populations decrease because of them?. 71

Why do some birds glide in flight, and others must flap constantly?. 73

Why do some birds at a feeder seem to throw away
   two or three seeds for every one they eat? 75

Why do some bird species seem to be expanding their
   range further to the north? 77

Why do birds fly? 79

Why do birds fluff their feathers and shiver in cold weather?. 81

Why do some birds do well in the city, and others do not? 83

Why do some birds appear only seasonally?. 85

Why do birds eat what they eat? 89

Why do some birds hop, others walk, and some run? 93

Why do birds chase, or fight, with each other?. 95

Like all plovers, the Black-bellied Plover (above) takes several small, rapid steps, then pauses. It can often be seen standing on one leg. The Mallard (opposite) is a "Dabbling Duck," or surface-feeding duck, meaning it primarily feeds on the water's surface by straining water through the bill.

Why do birds stand on one leg?

Humans may find standing on one leg not only awkward, but downright tiring. Our center of gravity is such that it is a struggle to maintain this stance for any length of time.

Not so with birds. They actually find standing on one leg relaxing. Because of the way they are built, they can balance easily on one leg. They often sleep this way. The flexor tendon in their leg actually "locks" onto the perch when tensioned, so even while sleeping, they are secure. Perching on one leg is thought to be an energy-saving adaptation.

One-leggedness may serve other purposes too. Herons and other wading birds often stand on one leg in the water while hunting. With only one leg visible underwater to fish and other creatures, it may appear as though the leg is just a reed or other natural object, putting the prey off guard. And perhaps these wading birds are lifting one leg just to let it dry off!

Additionally, standing on one leg probably helps with regulating body temperature, allowing the bird to tuck one foot up against, or even within, its feathers. This behavior is done in both cool weather and warm.

Why aren't birds electrocuted when they sit on wires?

Birds perch on wires for the same reasons they perch on tree limbs – they're comfortable places to rest that provides excellent visibility. Being able to see well is important for several reasons. For most songbirds, it is a means of defense. They can see avian predators from the high perch, and are safe from ground dwelling ones. They can also scan for potential food sources from on high.

The bigger question is why don't they get electrocuted while sitting on those electrical wires?

Besides the fact that most wires today have sufficient insulation to protect birds, the answer is simple: there isn't a completed circuit. In order for a bird (or you!) to get electrocuted, it must touch both a charged wire, and a grounding point, such as the ground, the top of the pole, or another wire, at the same time.

For the typical songbird, touching a wire and any of these other objects simultaneously is virtually impossible because of the bird's small size. Occasionally a large raptor, such as an eagle or large owl, does manage to create such a deadly circuit, but these events are quite rare.

The Purple Martin (opposite) is our largest swallow, and they can often be seen lined up on high, open wires by the hundreds or even thousands. Bronzed Cowbirds (right) also form dense flocks.

The loud, bubbling and complex song of the Bobolink (above) is more typical of birds in open country, where simple sustained vocalizations tend to be distorted by the wind and changes in air temperature common in grassland. The Northern Parula Warbler (opposite), like many wood warblers, gives a somewhat different song depending on the stage of the breeding cycle, the time of day, and the occasion.

Why do birds sing, and why mostly in the morning?

Let's answer the second half, first: birds sing mostly in the morning either to delight you, or to annoy you by waking you up.

Just kidding. Birds sing mostly in the morning for a couple of reasons. During the night, birds can become separated from their flock, so singing helps attract stragglers back. Birds also sing largely for reproductive purposes – to attract a mate or define a territory. The rising of the sun triggers these responses. For many species of birds, the greatest amount of mate calling, and territorial defense, occurs in the hour just before and the hour just after the sun appears.

There are other good reasons to sing, too. Many songbirds group in large flocks, which have a social order. Vocalizations tend to help shape, or reinforce, the "pecking" order.

Each bird species makes a variety of sounds that it uses to communicate with other birds: the often lyrical and frequently intricate songs, and the usually terse and simple calls. Birds rarely sing near their nests (it would attract predators) but young birds do sometimes call to remind their parents

that they are hungry. Other calls alert members of a flock either to danger, or to a good place to feed.

Few birds, except Northern Cardinals, sing in the winter. Most singing is done in the spring, and most of that is done by the males, often from atop a conspicuous perch in hopes of attracting the ladies and driving off rivals. Some species, such as larks and buntings, are known to sing on the wing.

Young birds don't know the songs of their species inherently. They learn them from adults, and it may take them a year to perfect the songs. A few species of birds have only one song, but some, like song sparrows, have as may as ten, and some wrens know one hundred!

Have you ever heard birds singing, and when you finally located the source, was surprised that there was only one bird instead of several? That's because many songbirds, thanks to separate windpipe muscles at the point where it branches to the two lungs, can alternate exhalations, and sing a duet with itself!

The Eastern Towhee (or Rufous-sided Towhee, opposite) male sings persistently from the beginning of the breeding season through various stages of nesting. Females of this species rarely sing. (above) Voice is probably the most reliable clue in identifying meadowlarks. Eastern males, like the one above, sing 50 to 100 songs, while Western males sing fewer than ten.

(Above and opposite) It has been estimated that there are close to 200 million Red-winged Blackbirds in North America. They form large winter flocks with other blackbirds in farmland and suburbs, and coalesce into massive roosting congregations at dusk.

Why do some birds fly as a flock?

Not all birds fly as a flock, but for those that do, there a several good reasons why.

Songbirds that flock together do so as a means of survival. Many eyes mean many early warning systems, increasing the odds that they will see a predator before the predator sees them. In addition, flocking birds (and herding animals) increase their odds of survival when a predator does attack, because as one part of a larger group, the odds of being the prey are reduced.

Similarly, many eyes are useful in spotting rewarding feeding opportunities, or good roosting and resting areas.

Many flocks, especially during migration, are comprised of several family groups. In this manner, young-of-the-year birds learn the routes necessary to travel safely to the wintering or nesting grounds.

Although it isn't practiced by songbirds, large birds, especially waterfowl like ducks and geese, fly in flocks not only for all the above reasons, but for the aerodynamic advantage of flying in the well-known "V" formation. Birds flying in this formation use as much as seventy percent less energy than were they to fly solo.

Waterfowl young are known for their heavy down and their precocity. Downy young, like these Wood Ducklings (above and opposite), cluster near one another as they hatch and demonstrate their bond as a brood by swimming in a tight group.

Why do some chicks hatch naked, and others hatch covered with down?

It is a curious thing that some birds hatch wrinkled and naked, while others sport a fluffy coat of down. You would think that what works for one bird species would work for all. But it doesn't.

Precocial young hatch with feathers (down) and eyes wide open, and often are able to leave the nest within hours of popping out of the egg. They are also able to feed themselves, usually by eating insects. Ducks, geese and shorebirds are examples of these kinds of birds.

Altricial young are naked and feeble. The songbirds you see in your backyard are examples of this kind of bird. The young are unable to feed themselves, or even leave the nest, so one or both parents must bring food to them.

The difference between the two is because of predation and food availability.

Birds, like ducks, that nest on the ground must have young that are mobile upon hatching, in order to avoid predators. Songbirds, which

mostly nest in trees or shrubs, are better defended from predators because of concealment.

Females of precocial species put great energy into laying nutrient-rich eggs, so that the young can emerge larger and more developed. That means they must have good access to high quality food before the eggs are laid. Typically, in these species, the male abandons the female after egg-laying, so she needs chicks that can feed themselves.

Altricial females don't need the pre-laying, up-front energy, but instead must be able to find abundant food after the eggs hatch in order to feed her nestlings. Males of these species usually remain with the female, and aid in finding food and feeding the young.

Both sexes of the Blue Grosbeak (opposite) feed the young for the 9 to 13 days until fledging. The female Wild Turkey (above) takes on the entire responsibility of incubation and brood-rearing, with the male taking no part.

Both the Northern Cardinal (above) and the American Goldfinch (left) have one to two, and occasionally three, broods per year.

Why do some birds have multiple broods per year?

Among songbirds, it is typical that they will produce only one brood per year. But as in all things in nature, there are exceptions.

Bluebirds, for instance, have been known to produce up to three broods in a single year. Chestnut-backed Chickadees are also known to produce several broods annually.

Another common bird, the Mourning Dove, also produces several broods in one year. So why do these birds continue to produce broods while others only produce one?

It is believed that producing multiple broods is simply another survival strategy. Every bird is driven to reproduce and pass on its own unique genetics. By producing more offspring, the odds of some of them surviving to adulthood and their own reproductive future increases.

There is also some evidence that the latitude at which the species nests has an influence in its propensity to produce more than one brood, largely because the growing season (both for food and for offspring) is longer.

Multiple broods are a different thing than "re-nesting." Many birds will lay a second clutch of eggs if the first clutch is destroyed early in the nesting cycle, and this second clutch is called "re-nesting." Sometimes, people think that these birds produced a second brood because they see young birds late in the summer, but this is not the case. The young birds are small late into the summer not because the female produced a second brood, but because the young are the result of a second attempt.

A female Northern Cardinal (above) and an American Robin (opposite) are shown taking water baths. This Gilded Flicker (right) is taking a dust bath.

Why do birds bathe?

It is believed that nearly all birds bathe, and they do so for the same reasons you and I do – to get clean.

A bird without healthy feathers is a bird in big trouble. As durable as feathers seem, they really are amazingly-complex features that require care. Preening, discussed elsewhere, is the bird's way of aligning its feathers. But preening would be largely pointless if the feathers were saturated with plant juices or dirt.

Hence, the bathing. Different species have different styles of bathing. For instance, swallows and swifts actually fly so low that they skim through the water's surface – sort of the bird version of a power wash.

Others, like Robins, nearly immerse themselves, throw water over their backs using their wings, and dip their heads, letting the water run down their necks. Water birds, like ducks and gulls, first dip under the water, then shake like a dog.

All of this is in an effort to remove dirt and debris from their feathers, as well as mites and other insects. If water isn't available, some birds will take a dust bath. While it seems counterintuitive to throw dirt on yourself to get clean, the fine dust that birds bathe in actually collects larger dirt particles, which can then be shaken out through rigorous shaking.

The Horned Grebe molts from a white basic plumage (top), suitable for life in the winter, to a cinnamon-brown alternate plumage (bottom) that provides more effective camouflage in its breeding vegetation during the summer months.

Why do birds molt?

Molting is the term used to refer to the process birds go through each year to replace worn feathers.

Not only do birds molt to replace old feathers, they do so to change entire plumages — for instance, from that of a sub-adult to an adult, or from their "knock around" every day clothes, to the "glad rags" of the breeding season. Other molts result in entirely different plumages for camouflage reasons; their winter colors may be white or drab to blend in with snow or drab tree colors, while their summer colors may be brighter to blend in with their breeding grounds.

Most birds molt just a few feathers at a time so that they are never flightless. The old feathers are pushed out by the new ones. A few species of birds, mostly waterfowl, actually are flightless during the molt, but most of these can escape predation by swimming into open water or hiding among reeds. Feathers don't grow more quickly for big birds than they do for small birds, so large birds, like eagles, must molt over the course of two years or they'd be unable to fly.

Small birds, such as songbirds, replace all of their flight feathers and body plumage annually, and sometimes twice. The first molt is after the breeding season (late summer or early fall), but for those songbirds that are brightly colored in the summer and duller in the winter, a second molt takes place.

Because molting demands a lot of energy, birds do it when they aren't doing other energy-intense things, such as laying eggs, breeding, or migrating.

The male Goldfinch has a bright yellow breeding plumage that can be seen throughout the summer (left), but wears a much duller winter plumage that helps him blend into the muted colors of winter (right).

Why do birds of the same species often look different in the spring than in the fall or winter?

In many bird species, there is a surplus of males, largely because the female's tasks of laying and incubating a clutch is dangerous. She must sit still for long periods of time in the face of predation and bad weather. Consequently, the mortality rate for females of some bird species is significantly higher than that of males.

So what's a guy to do if he's faced with lots of competition? The answer to that question is that he tries to get noticed and stand out from the crowd, and one way male birds do that is to grow new plumage that is brighter and more colorful than at any other time of year in order to attract a mate.

Females generally select the male, not the other way around, so a male must convince a female that he's the best mate around. He does that in several ways – through possessing a good territory, making a variety of vocalizations, and through ritual display. But the most obvious "come-on" (at least to us as we observe them) is his bright, nuptial plumage.

Depending on the species, males adopt these colors from mid-winter to as late as March. But no matter when it occurs, it always takes place before pair selection gets really serious. Not only do the males of some species get brighter in color, the actual pattern of the plumage may be different than during the rest of the year.

And what about the females? Those of some species actually do sport a little brighter (though no change in pattern) plumage during the courtship stage, but resume drabber, more camouflaged coloration for the breeding season.

The Loggerhead Shrike's (top left) normal diet is insects, but its strong, hooked bill is also used to kill and dismember prey much larger than itself; the Great Blue Heron (top right) hunts fish and other animals while wading slowly in shallow water; the unique bill of the Red Crossbill (bottom right) is used to pry out the seeds of the cones of pines, spruces, and firs; the Northern Cardinal (bottom left) has a thick, conical bill perfect for cracking seeds; and the Brown Pelican's bill (opposite) is ideal for scooping up its fish diet.

Why do bird beaks come in so many shapes and sizes?

If you want to do the job right, then choose the right tool – or so the saying goes.

It is no different for birds. Since birds have evolved to fit almost every imaginable niche and food source, their beaks have become specialized, largely based on diet.

Cardinals have thick, stout bills designed to crack open larger seeds and nuts, a favorite food. Their beaks are like pliers. The Robin, however, is a generalist in diet. She'll eat everything from fruit, to worms, to insects. Consequently, the Robin's bill is specialized only in the sense that it is a sort of all-around tool – the Swiss Army Knife of beaks.

Woodpeckers, of course, have very specialized "jack-hammer" beaks to drill away at rotting wood where they find the insects they eat. Hummingbirds have long slender bills designed to slip into flowers to "vacuum" up nectar. And birds of prey have bills that tear and shear, so they can dismember and eat the birds, fish, and mammals they catch. There are even birds, like the Northern Shoveler duck, that have broad bills with extremely fine filters inside that allow them to skim water and filter out tiny microscopic invertebrates.

So why so many shapes and sizes? Specialized diets and habitats have shaped the bird's beak over eons of evolution.

This Red-shouldered Hawk (above) is using its bill to smooth the vanes of its tail feathers, while the Sandhill Crane (opposite) is busy caring for its shoulder feathers. Preening is a daily chore for all birds, and with the number of feathers on a bird's body ranging from around 1,000 on hummingbirds to more than 25,000 on swans, you can imagine how much of a daily chore it is!

Why do birds preen?

Preening – the care of feathers – is one of the most important things birds do for themselves. After all, feathers are of the utmost importance to birds, allowing them to fly, to be camouflaged, and to insulate them (most birds have a body temperature of about 104° Fahrenheit, which feathers help them maintain). Without preening, feathers would wear out prematurely.

Birds preen themselves by stroking their feathers – pulling them through their bills. This helps to realign the barbs of the feathers so that they are less likely to get broken, and so the feathers lie smoothly on the bird, providing better insulation and better aerodynamics.

It may even appear to you that the bird is nibbling on its feathers. It is. Stubborn places require more effort to get the barbs (which are Velcro-like) realigned.

Birds also apply oil from a special gland during preening. This oil keeps feathers from drying out and becoming brittle, and also helps waterfowl stay waterproof.

The ruff-out display of the Red-Winged Blackbird (left) is a common sight in spring over most of North America. This display is used in territorial defense rather than to attract females.

The Prothonotary Warbler (below) has one primary song type per male (thought to act as mate attraction), and a second, more complex extended song that is believed to be used in territorial defense.

Why do birds establish territories?

Birds establish territories in order to increase the odds of their own survival, and the survival of their young.

Territory size varies considerably among species, but no matter the kind of bird, the attributes are much the same. Territories give birds a place to carry on courtship and mating, and often include exclusive rights to food sources. In songbirds, the rights to food sources is less pronounced, since they will often share space at backyard feeders, but their territories will always be located near good feeding opportunities, shared or not.

In social birds that nest near each other, the territory may be no larger than the nest site, plus a few feet of space surrounding it. Large raptors, like bald eagles, may have a territory of many miles. Songbirds tend to have small territories that may include your backyard and that of your neighbor. In any case, these territories are defended by the male, and even sometimes by the female. It is important to the mated pair to have a resource to call their own, because from it they must not only meet their own physical needs, but those of their offspring. Territories also help disperse birds across available habitat, avoiding competition that would lower survival rates if all were congregated.

Some birds also defend food sources. No doubt you've witnessed hummingbirds chasing each other around your hummingbird feeder. This activity seems to peak during the breeding season, when the energy needs of breeding adults are high.

It is easy to distinguish the males and females of many species simply by their plumage. Good examples are the Northern Cardinal (above) and the Eastern Bluebird (opposite). In both species, the males are much brighter and more brilliantly colored.

Why do male birds have brighter colors than females?

Although there are bird species in which the males and females are virtually identical in appearance, in most species, males are considerably more colorful than females. Why?

Females have much more muted colors – called cryptic coloration – because they do the egg laying and incubation. Both exercises require her to spend a great deal of time sitting still, even in the face of dangers, such as predation. In order to remain unseen, females have evolved nicely camouflaged appearances.

Males, however, have different requirements. First, they must attract a mate, since it is the female that usually does the selecting. Males sport bright colors in an effort to lure a mate, and females use the quality of his plumage as a visual indicator of his fitness. Males must also defend their territo-ries, and bright colors make them visible to rivals, and may even act as an intimidating factor.

In most species, males don't attain their complete bright plumage until their first winter. Until then, they look much like their mothers, which makes identifying immature males difficult.

Why do birds migrate?

Migration, while fascinating to us, is nothing more than yet another wonderful survival strategy of birds. While some birds do live year round in the region they were born (although making some short, seasonal movements), most northern birds must migrate to survive.

So why do birds go north to nest? Northern habitats, though stark in winter, are often lush with foods during the time birds need energy the most – the breeding season – because the growing season in northern latitudes is so compressed. This fast-paced growing season gives female birds the needed nutrients and energy to produce eggs, and also provides plentiful food for hatchlings to grow quickly.

In autumn, birds migrate south as far as needed to find food and a secure wintering habitat. How far they travel is all relative. For some, like the Ruby-throated Hummingbird, that may mean migrating from southern Canada to South America. For others, like the Bohemian Waxwing, which nests in Alaska and the Northwest Territories of Canada, migrating only as far south as Minnesota is enough to secure needed food.

Of course, not all birds migrate, even if they live in the north. Black-capped Chickadees are year round residents in the north, being well adapted to winter's rigors.

Sandhill Cranes (opposite) migrate thousands of miles each year. Most fly at altitudes of 500 to 2,500 feet, and typically fly in a V formation once they've reached their "cruising" altitude. In this V formation, they can fly/glide up to 500 miles in nine or ten hours.

Most large soaring birds, like the Red-tailed Hawk (top left) have long, narrow outer primaries that allow the birds to fly at slower speeds without stalling. Hummingbirds (Anna's Hummingbird shown, top right) have the unique ability to hover and even to fly backward. The Prairie Falcon (bottom right) has long, pointed wings that allow for incredible speed and twisting maneuverability. The Purple Martin (bottom left) also has long, pointed wings that allow it to forage for aerial insects in wide, swooping flight.

Why do some birds have short, broad wings, and others have long, tapered wings?

Wing shape reveals a lot about how a bird lives, and those shapes are based on habitat and feeding styles. Short, broad-winged birds typically are forest dwellers, who frequently feed on the ground, and who must be able to make tight twists and turns through tree limbs. These kinds of wings also allow birds to burst directly into the air from the ground or from a perch. Most songbirds, such as warblers, have wings of this type. Wingtips are typically fairly rounded, though flexible, with slots between feathers, so that they can be individually adjusted without twisting the whole wing.

Some common birds, like swifts and swallows, have a wing designed for high-speed aerial acrobatics. Because they feed on flying insects, they are the "fighter jets" of the bird world. Their wings are flat, moderately long, triangular in shape, lack the slots, and can be swept back. Some small raptors, like the falcons, which also feed in the air (on both insects and slower birds) have similar wing shapes.

Of all the birds that come to your feeder, the hummingbird has the most specialized wings. Their wings are pointed and swept back, and do not rotate at the "wrist" as do most birds' wings, but at the shoulder. When in flight, the shoulder rotation allows them to actually turn their wings over — the forward stroke cancels the backward stroke, allowing for true hovering in place.

The Blue Grosbeak (above) eats mainly seeds during the non-breeding season, and insects and fruit during the breeding season. The Great Crested Flycatcher (opposite) catches flying insects in midair, often returning to perch with its prey.

Why do birds seem to eat constantly?

Because they do! Birds have an extremely high metabolic rate, which requires large amounts of food relative to body size. For instance, the hummingbird, with its rapid wing beats, has a metabolic rate almost 100 times greater than that of an elephant!

Consequently, it must eat one and a half to three times its own body weight per day.

Another reason birds must eat nearly all the time is because they have a very short period of time to grow up. In other words, a hatchling born in May has only until September to grow large enough to make its first migration. Typically, young birds eat a lot of insects, even if their species is largely a seed-eating type, because insects are high in protein and provide the fuel needed to get to flight stage, called fledging.

Finally, birds eat so much because they must molt (replace feathers), which requires far more energy than growing hair or fur does for mammals. Additionally, though flight is a very efficient means of travel, it demands a lot of fuel.

The male Wild Turkey (left) is heavily ornamented, all to help it attract a mate. Male Ruffed Grouse (opposite) use a thumping display to attract females; once a female is in sight, the male begins a more elaborate posturing display (shown in photo).

Why do male birds "strut their stuff" during mating season?

It's not easy being a male bird. Usually, males outnumber the females, so there is a lot of competition for a mate. Males are also largely responsible for establishing a territory in which his mate can incubate eggs and where they can rear their young. And it is usually the male's job to defend this territory from interlopers of either sex that seek to displace him and his mate.

With all this going on, it is important that male birds be fine specimens. If they aren't, their mates and offspring will suffer the consequences. Because it is generally the female who chooses the male, she needs a means of evaluating his fitness. A bird's plumage is one way that they communicate this – a finely feathered male, decked out in his brightest colors, indicates he is mature, and thus is

a survivor. His song is another means of assessing his virility.

Birds also convey fitness through movement. The male Wild Turkey, Ruffed Grouse, and other similar birds, go through ritualistic chest puffing and strutting or dancing in order to convince females that they have the right stuff. Songbirds more often perform a less dramatic show, usually flashing some of their more striking plumage on tails or wings, which serves not only to attract females, but is thought to intimidate rival males.

These Eastern Bluebird eggs will all hatch at approximately the same time, even though each egg was laid at least one day apart.

Why do eggs hatch all at the same time, even when laid days apart?

One of the most fascinating things about birds is their reproductive cycle. One of the greatest mysteries about it is how, when eggs are laid hours or even days apart, do they happen to hatch all at the same time?

First, it is important that they do hatch together, since any hatchlings that came a day or two earlier, because of the rapid rate at which birds grow, would have a real competitive advantage over its cohorts. In addition, once the chicks hatch, the female's role needs to change from one of incubator, to that of food provider. Having to sit on some eggs while also feeding other hatchlings would be too difficult to do.

So birds have developed the remarkable ability to coordinate hatch times. Freshly-laid eggs are remarkably cold tolerant, so initially she doesn't need to keep them warm. In fact, if she began incubating as soon as the first egg were laid, that egg would hatch many days before the last egg. By waiting to incubate until the last egg is laid, the eggs hatch synchronously.

One last thing is thought to occur – chicks of some species start to chirp or peep a day or so before hatching and scrape their "egg tooth" (a temporary knob on the top of their beak used to help break the egg shell open for hatching) on the shell. It is speculated that this form of communication helps the chicks synchronize their emergence.

This Blue-winged Warbler (above) is apparently unable to detect that it is feeding a Brown-headed Cowbird fledgling. Such "hosts" are called "acceptor" species. Similarly, there is a cowbird nestling (larger bird on left) sharing the nest with Kentucky Warbler nestlings in the photo to the left. Brown-headed and Shiny Cowbirds each have been reported to parasitize more than 200 species.

Why do some birds "dump" their eggs in the nests of other birds, even birds of other species?

Called "egg dumping" or "brood parasitism," this is the behavior in which the female lays eggs in the nest of another of her own species, or even in the nest of a completely different species. A good indicator that this has happened is if two new eggs appear in a nest in one day, since few birds lay more than one egg in a day.

One of the most infamous egg-dumpers is the North American cowbird. Not only do they dump eggs in the nests of other birds, they don't even build their own nest. The Brown-headed Cowbird has been recorded as a parasite of more than 200 other species. If they lay their eggs in the nest of smaller birds, the hatchling cowbirds not only hatch sooner, but have a competitive size advantage, and so cause the deaths of the natural offspring. This behavior has been documented as having a serious impact on the populations of Kirkland's Warblers and Black-capped Vireos.

Cliff Swallows are another parasitic bird, but they lay their eggs in the nests of neighbors of their own species. Sometimes, they'll even toss out their neighbor's eggs in order to replace them with their own.

What happens when a female notices mysterious eggs in her nest? Robins, which lay blue eggs, frequently recognize the spotted cowbird eggs as foreign, and so toss them out. The Song Sparrow, though, lays eggs similar in size and color of the cowbird, so frequently ends up incubating them.

Of the more than 650 bird species that nest in North America, 75 percent partake in some form of migration. Waterfowl are species commonly seen migrating, and high altitude migration is especially common in geese. There are records of Snow Geese (above) observed flying at 20,000 feet during migration, and Canadas (opposite) regularly move over land areas at altitudes of 1,000 to 5,000 feet.

Why do birds seem to know their way during migration?

Migrating birds seem to know their way during migration because they actually do!

Few things have intrigued humans more about birds than their ability to travel great distances unerringly. Many North American birds, for instance, migrate the length of the continent, and a few migrate to South America.

Migration "knowledge" seems to have two basis. One is learned. Young birds often learn migration routes from parents or from older members of their flock.

The other knowledge factor is their ability to navigate. Studies have shown that pigeon's have a small amount of iron-bearing matter in their brains, which has caused scientists to speculate that they (and probably other bird species) are sensitive to the earth's magnetic poles. This is reinforced by the fact that birds can and do migrate in the fog or on cloudy days or nights when getting bearings from celestial bodies would be impossible. A most recent study indicated that birds orient themselves with the sunset, which of course is always in the west, thus setting them up for the next leg of travel.

Additionally, birds probably also use visual clues, such as rivers and other landmarks to find their way.

The Ovenbird (top left) nests on the ground and constructs a dome of grass stems and leaves over the nest. The Least Tern (bottom left) is a beach-nesting bird, laying its eggs directly on the ground. Camouflaged eggs are what keep them safe from predators. Constructed almost entirely by the female, the White-eyed Vireo (bottom right) builds a well-formed, hanging, open-cup nest made of grasses, leaf and bark fibers, and spider silk.

Why do some birds nest in trees, while others nest on the ground?

Since it is believed that birds long ago evolved from reptiles, which are also egg layers, it is likely that in the beginning, all birds laid their eggs on the ground. This strategy, however, has its problems, most notably that eggs and nests on the ground are easier for predators to find.

Songbirds invariably nest in trees and bushes, which provides a much greater measure of protection and concealment. But some common birds continue to nest on the ground, such as Ovenbirds and Killdeer, and they've evolved their own adaptations to the predation problem.

Ovenbirds hide their eggs beneath the leaves and forest floor debris in mounds that resemble a Dutch Oven, hence their name. Killdeer barely scrape out a depression in gravel, but

their eggs so perfectly match the ground in coloration, that they are nearly impossible to see. When a predator appears, the Killdeer departs, so that it doesn't act as a marker of the nest's location. The Killdeer also often pretends to have an injured wing and lures predators away from the nest with this ruse. When the predator has been led far enough away from the nest, the adult flies off.

A few birds are so large that they can defend themselves and their nest. The Canada Goose, now so common across the United States, is big enough to drive off just about any predator. In addition, a pair remains together through the nesting season, and two Canada Geese are simply too intimidating for most predators.

The Belted Kingfisher (above) hunts small fish, crustaceans, aquatic insects, reptiles and amphibians in streams, rivers, freshwater ponds and lakes. They hunt by sight and require clear water to find prey. They also live a solitary life when not breeding. In contrast, White-crowned Sparrows (opposite) flock together to forage for food and can often be seen in bushes and other cover in large numbers.

Why do some birds live solitary lives, while others flock together?

Forming into flocks is thought to be a strategy that allows birds to be safer. Many eyes allows for quicker spotting of predators, and one bird among many is much more likely to survive an attack on the flock.

In addition, birds flock together as an aid in teaching and rearing young. Although by the time fall rolls around, young birds may be nearly indistinguishable from adults, they have much to learn, including migration routes. Flocks are often groups of families that have joined together, and even though the parental bonds to their own young have become weak by autumn, the young birds, now as full members of the flock, continue to learn about food sources, survival, and travel routes. Flocking birds almost always depend on foods that are found in large quantities in a small area — such as gulls feeding on bait fish, or Cedar Waxwings chowing down in a fruit-laden bush.

In flight, flocking may also provide some aerodynamic benefits, especially for those species that fly in tight "V" formation.

Solitary birds tend to be hunters. A Great Blue Heron could not easily survive in a flock, because its prey, such as frogs or salamanders, are widely dispersed. Hawks, eagles, and owls are other good examples of solitary birds.

Pair bonds vary greatly among ducks and geese. Geese, such as these Canadas (left), have long pair bonds that often last for life, and both sexes share in brood care. Both sexes of the Red-shouldered Hawk (opposite) incubate the eggs. Females do most of the chick-feeding once the young are hatched, while males do most of the hunting and bring food to the nest.

Horned Grebes (right) share many characteristics with loons. In both species, both adults tend the young in sheltered waters and carry the chicks on their backs.

Why do males of some species stay with the female and their young, while in other species, the male departs?

Whether or not the male remains with his mate after the eggs are laid largely depends on whether the pair is about to raise precocial or altricial chicks.

Precocial chicks are born with down, are able to leave the nest within hours, and can feed themselves. The familiar Mallard Duck is an example of a bird who has precocial chicks. Altricial chicks are hatched naked and helpless, often barely able to lift their heads. These are the kinds of chicks most songbirds and raptors raise.

Precocial chicks feed themselves, and learn all they need to know from their mother. Since the father isn't needed for feeding duties, he departs. In fact, if he hung around, he'd just be competing with them for food. Males of these species tend to congregate in bachelor groups in habitats their young won't be needing after their mate begins incubation.

Altricial chicks are so helpless, they require the feeding efforts and protection of both parents. Unable to feed themselves, yet needing to grow quickly, these chicks demand the presence of two parents to keep them in groceries.

Why do some birds mate for life?

Actually, very few birds do mate for life, and none of them are songbirds. Eagles and Canada Geese are two of the most familiar bird species that form life-long pair bonds (although if one dies, they'll find another mate, and they sometimes "divorce" because of incompatibility).

Most songbirds, however, are socially monogamous. That means that upon forming a pair bond, they will remain together throughout the breeding and nesting season.

But even monogamous birds can be "naughty." Recent studies that use genetic testing show that there's a whole lot of what scientists call "extra-pair copulations," or what you and I would call "cheating on our spouse" happening. By taking a small sample of blood, scientists can tell whether the offspring in the nest are indeed the offspring of the male of the pair. If they are, then the pair is considered "genetically monogamous." If not, they are "socially monogamous" (which means they remain together despite the cheating!).

And what have these peeping-Tom scientists found? That apparently, genetic monogamy is the exception, rather than the rule. It is believed that females choose to mate with other males in order to hedge their bet against possible infertility of her chosen mate. Birds have short lifespans, and if she is going to insure she passes on her genes, she can't afford to go through a breeding season without producing offspring.

A Bald Eagle pair (opposite) often mates for life. They typically use the same nest for years. These nests can become huge, weighing hundreds of pounds and being many feet thick.

All birds can reduce heat loss by constricting the flow of warm blood through the leg arteries into exposed feet and legs. Birds can reduce heat loss in their extremities by up to 90 percent, which allows Northern Mockingbirds (above) and Pintail Ducks (opposite) to stand on snowy branches and icy water without losing too much body heat.

Why do the feet of birds not freeze in extreme cold?

A bird's feet don't freeze largely because there is very little to freeze! A bird's legs are made of mostly scales, bones and sinews, with the real muscles up in the well-feathered thighs (think of a turkey drumstick – the part of the bird leg you most often see is the part that has been lopped off below the knuckle on the drumstick).

Birds also have minimal blood flow to their feet, so while their body temperature may be over 100 degrees, their feet can be near the freezing point. If your feet were that cold, you'd swear they were frozen, but for birds, this is not a hardship.

Additionally, some birds have what is called "counter current heat exchange." This term is just fancy scientist talk for the fact that the arteries and veins in bird legs are right next to each other. As blood flows down the legs in the arteries from the warmer body, it meets up with colder blood coming back up in the veins. The warmth from the arteries warms up the blood in the veins before the venous blood reenters the body, thus keeping the bird's body warm.

Ducks such as these American Black Ducks, American Wigeons, and Mallards (above) typically hunker down when prey flies overhead. Quails like the Northern Bobwhite Quail (opposite) are usually quite secretive and will stay motionless on the ground until a predator is very close. Then its explosive take-off surprises the predator as the bird flies away.

Why do some birds hunker down when an avian predator flies overhead, while others erupt into flight?

Whether or not a bird hunkers down and hides, or erupts into flight when an avian predator appears largely depends on how the bird is built.

In other words, if the bird is slow on the wing, it is better off hiding on the ground. But if it is swift and able to make fine maneuvers in the air, then it stands a better chance trying to out-fly the hawk or falcon.

Sometimes, the same bird may use both strategies, depending on the situation. If a chickadee thinks it can reach the dense cover of some bushes before the Sharp-shinned Hawk can catch it, it will flush. But if it is caught with its guard down, and it is too late to flee, it will hold still. Water birds, such as ducks when caught on land, will often flush, but if in the water,

will remain there because they can always dive under to avoid an eagle or other predator.

These behaviors, it seems, are instinctive and not learned. In order to test this, researchers took pen-raised quail that had never before seen a hawk, and placed them in the open. When exposed to a raptor, they instantly hunkered down.

The American Goldfinch and Black-capped Chickadee (left) are often seen in backyards and at feeders together because they share a similar diet. Similarly, White-crowned Sparrows and Golden-crowned Sparrows (opposite) are also often seen flocking together.

Why do birds of different species sometimes flock and feed together?

It isn't at all unusual to see birds of several species feeding together at the same location. And although it isn't quite as common, it also isn't unheard of that birds of different species will even fly together in flocks.

The reasons for these mixed flocks are protection and better food utilization. Near-sighted birds, such as vireos, sometimes feed with sharper-vision flycatchers, which help to act as sentinels. It's been shown through experiments that Downy Woodpeckers often associate with the alert Black-capped Chickadee for exactly the same reason.

Some scientists believe that mixed flocks tend to be more efficient feeders. Birds of similar species with similar diets learn about new foods from each other. Having more birds together also is thought to increase the likelihood of finding good food sources.

In flocks where the birds don't have similar diets, birds still gain the benefit of protection from predators, yet are not faced with as much competition for food as they would be if they were feeding in a flock comprised of birds of their own species.

Mixed species flocks are most often seen during migration and other non-breeding periods.

The Barred Owl (above) and the Eastern Screech-Owl (opposite) are incredible night hunters. Most owls spend the daytime concealed in vegetation or cavities, with eyes closed and body feathers compressed to blend in with tree bark. At night, however, their eyes become wide open and their body feathers relax as they perch and hunt for prey.

Why do some birds hunt at night, and others in the day?

Just as ground-dwelling animals tend to be divided by whether they are creatures of the night or day, so too are birds.

Most birds, including most song-birds, are *diurnal*, which means they are most active at dusk and dawn, and that's when they do the bulk of their feeding. But the birds that prey on them or on mammals are either day hunters or night hunters.

Hawks, in particular, are daytime hunters. Because they soar – glide along on updrafts – while watching for prey, they must wait for the day to begin to warm, so that the uplifting thermals have formed. Falcons are less dependent on thermals than hawks, and hunt most often when their prey – other birds – are active.

But owls are truly creatures of the night. With their large eyes and incredible night vision, they perch in trees, watching for mammals or roost-ing birds. They don't need thermals at all, because they glide down on silent wings when snatching their prey. Thus, they can hunt at night when cool air inhibits updrafts. They also hunt at night because they have evolved to be perfectly adapted to the darkness, and face no other avian competition.

American Robins (above and opposite) routinely cock their heads from side to side. Research has shown that this behavior is a form of visual hunting; they stand upright with their head cocked to watch for prey, then hop forward when they see it. While it looks like the Robin is listening for prey (usually worms), it is actually looking for it.

Why do ground feeding birds, like the American Robin, cock their heads to the side?

The fact that we hear — and enjoy — bird song is a good indicator that the range of hearing for birds is very much like ours. They wouldn't be making sounds that other birds couldn't hear.

That doesn't mean that their hearing isn't superior to ours — humans process sounds in bytes about 1/20 of a second long whereas birds discriminate up to 1/200 of a second! A bird may hear ten distinct notes in a song, while we hear only one. Pigeons, and some other birds, can hear much lower sounds than us, and owls, which have one ear lower than the other, actually have a sort of "binocular" hearing that helps them pinpoint prey.

So why do birds cock their heads? Although the internal mechanism of bird ears is very similar to that of mammals, they lack the external fleshy part, which helps direct sound waves into the auditory canal. By cocking their heads, they can point an ear toward the source of the sound.

In the Robin's case, however, there is some belief that he is actually visually hunting rather than listening for prey although he might be doing both. Other thrushes that forage on the ground display the same behavior, such as plovers. So a Robin cocking his head might be listening for those worms, and looking for them too.

As opportunists, American Crows (above and opposite) take advantage of any available food source. Crows are especially adaptable to the urban landscape, often frequenting dumpsters, compost piles, and other sources of waste food.

Why do crows move into human neighborhoods, and why do some songbird populations decrease because of them?

Crows have been moving into urban areas in recent years in ever-increasing numbers, largely because we've made it easy for them to do so. Crows are great scavengers, and the trash and litter humans are prone to spreading provides forage.

Crows raise a brood of three or four hatchlings, which grow quickly to a large size. In order to grow so quickly, they need a lot of protein, and that protein often comes in the form of songbird eggs or hatchlings.

Songbird adults are pretty much immune to crow attacks, but their helpless young are not. Small birds species that nest on tiny branches in dense shrubbery escape crow attacks because the limbs are too small to hold a crow. But larger songbirds, such as robins, blackbirds and jays, tend to nest in sturdier places, where crows can easily pluck out eggs or chicks.

So do crows cause declines in songbirds? The jury is out. The birds they most often prey on, such as robins, are still very abundant. And some ornithologists believe that the watchful eye of the crow, which is quick to spot avian predators and stalking cats, and follow up with a raucous warning call, actually alert other birds to danger.

Why do some birds glide in flight, and others must flap constantly?

Bird wings come in varying shapes, and each shape is specialized for certain types of flight. Why some birds must flap, and others can easily glide or soar, has to do with *aspect ratio* and *wing loading*.

Aspect ratio describes variation in wing shape by looking at the ratio of the wing length to its width. A long, narrow wing (great for gliding) has a high aspect ratio, while a wing of similar length and width has a low aspect ratio. Birds with low aspect ratios have to flap frequently to stay airborne.

Hummingbirds, like the Broad-billed Hummingbird shown (top left), flap their wings so quickly they produce a humming sound. Turkey Vultures (top right) soar long distances searching for carrion, and can be identified in flight by the V-shape of their wings. Bald Eagles (bottom left) can be identified in flight by their nearly flat wingspan. Like most songbirds, the Carolina Chickadee (bottom right) can quickly take off from any perch.

Wing loading is a term that describes why birds with similar wing shapes fly differently. Wing loading is the relationship between total body mass and total wing area. What this means is that if two different species both have the same type of wing shape but have different body masses (one large, one small), and possess about the same wing size, the smaller bird will have less wing loading – and will be able to fly and glide more effortlessly.

Almost all songbirds have low aspect ratio – good for quick takeoffs, but poor for gliding. Wading birds, such as sandpipers, have a medium aspect ratio. They can take off fairly quickly, but can also glide well. The best gliders have high aspect ratio, such as eagles and vultures.

This Red-bellied Woodpecker (above) has found a peanut in a tray of sunflower seeds, while the Carolina Chickadee (opposite) will take its sunflower seed back to a perch for cracking and eating.

Why do some birds at a feeder seem to throw away two or three seeds for every one they eat?

The beak of a bird is a highly specialized tool. Each species of bird has its own environmental niche, within which they frequently select very specific foods. Their beaks are designed to best utilize those foods.

But at feeders, the food is anything but natural, and is often larger or smaller than that which they would find in the wild.

When birds grab food, they manipulate it – they turn it in order to make swallowing easier. In the process, they may drop a seed unintentionally, which makes it seem like they are tossing it away.

But sometimes they do toss it away. If the seed is too large, away it goes. And if it is has too hard a shell to crack, the same thing may happen. Many kinds of birds dine at our feeders, but the food source is pretty uniform, so each will have different ways of handling it. Some species, like grosbeaks or cardinals, with heavy, seed-cracking bills, may be less proficient at opening softer or smaller seeds, and so drop them. Thin-billed birds, such as Pine Siskins, are much more adept at small seeds, like that of thistle, but need to rummage through sunflower seeds to select the smaller ones they can open.

The Northern Cardinal (above) has always stayed year-round in its breeding range, but they are starting to be seen more frequently in even more northerly regions. This Northern Mockingbird (opposite) is adaptable to occasional snowfalls.

Why do some bird species seem to be expanding their range further to the north?

In the last few decades, a number of bird species have spread north of what has always been considered their core breeding areas. Cardinals, Clay-colored Sparrows, Great-tailed and Boat-tailed Grackles, and the Tufted Titmouse are all examples of species whose range has moved north, sometimes dramatically.

There are several reasons why such expansion is occurring. Changes in habitat – such as the conversion of the prairies to farmland – has encouraged the two grackles to greatly expand their range.

Climate change is another reason birds are changing their range. The extraordinarily warm winters in the last decade have made it possible for cold-intolerant species to expand their ranges, not only because the temperatures are more favorable, but because snow cover is more intermittent, thanks to sporadic warm spells. This allows birds to forage in regions formerly covered by snow.

It is also believed that the enormous amount of backyard feeding taking place could also be playing a roll in expanding bird ranges. The feeders provide food sources that make it possible for some species to move into regions where their natural food does not exist.

The ability to fly, the beautiful range of feathers and unique appearances, and the diversity of bird species may be why we are so fascinated by them. Each bird is beautiful and perfectly adapted to its own niche, including the Eastern Bluebird (left), the Osprey (bottom left), the Mallard (bottom right), and the Great Egret (opposite).

Why do birds fly?

We know an awful lot about how birds fly, but the question *why do they fly?* goes largely unanswered. We can speculate, however. It is easy to imagine several good reasons for flight: to help escape from predators; to help catch speedy prey; to make it easier to move from place to place; and to make it possible to get at food sources or a niche not occupied by other species.

The earliest known bird is the *Archaeopteryx*, which lived about 150 million years ago, and is sort of an intermediate between the birds that we see flying and predatory dinosaurs. Based on wing shape and body size, it probably wasn't a powerful flyer or a particularly good glider. But, as birds evolved from this species, they gradually increased their flying ability.

So why do birds fly? Because they can! It is an amazing adaptation, but it may forever remain a mystery why long ago, some creature we would not today recognize as a bird, began to evolve towards flight. Perhaps it was a small, bipedal dinosaur that captured prey by leaping, and who developed small wing-ish forelimbs to aid in expanding the length of its leaps?

In any case, today's 9,000 worldwide bird species show many variations of flight, from the flightless penguin to the acrobatic swallow, and are the most diverse group of flyers ever to exist.

Both this Dark-eyed Junco (top) and Rufous-sided Towhee (bottom) are fluffed up against the cold. Feathers provide better insulation than mammalian hair. When resting, a bird can tuck its head and feet into its feathers to conserve even more heat.

Why do birds fluff their feathers and shiver in cold weather?

Fluffing up their feathers and shivering are the two best adaptations birds have evolved to survive cold weather.

Many feathers have significant insulation properties, and fluffing them increases the dead-air space between the feathers and the skin. It is the original "down jacket." More dead-air means more warm air is trapped, which retains body heat. Simply by fluffing their feathers, a bird can increase its heat retention by up to 30 percent.

Birds actually grow more feathers in the winter to help with this, too. A chickadee has about 1,000 feathers in the summer, but by winter, it will have around 2,000. The more feathers, the more fluffing up they can do!

Additionally, birds shiver – a lot. In fact, they shiver almost constantly in the winter. Unlike us, where shivering is an uncomfortable feeling, the bird uses shivering to increase its body temperature. This shivering process is called *thermogenosis*. The constant shivering produces heat five times that of their normal rate, helping them to maintain their amazingly high body temperature.

Of course, all that shivering burns a lot of calories. Birds store the needed calories just like you and I do – as fat. But they can't store much. It is thought that birds are capable of only storing a reserve that will last them less than twenty-four hours, which is why, as soon as the cold winter night has ended, birds flock to your feeders to stoke up again.

The Rock Dove, or Common Pigeon (top left), and the Chipping Sparrow (top right) thrive in cities and towns. Chimney Swifts (bottom) have found perfect nesting cavities in people's chimneys. Because they cannot perch, but cling to vertical surfaces at nest and roost sites, chimneys are a perfect adaptation for them. In the wild, Chimney Swifts nest and roost in hollow trees.

Why do some birds do well in the city, and others do not?

Over the last hundred years or so, large cities and their surrounding housing suburbs have grown, replacing countryside habitats. Many species of birds have disappeared from such areas, but a few birds have adapted themselves to the man-made environment.

Some of the birds most commonly found in cities, towns, and suburbs include: Herring Gull, Mourning Dove, Rock Dove (Pigeon), Common Crow, Bluejay, Black-capped Chickadee, Red-breasted Nuthatch, Northern Mockingbird, American Robin, Yellow Warbler, European Starling, House Sparrow, Northern Cardinal, Chipping Sparrow, and Song Sparrow.

The artificial concrete and steel ecosystems of cities, including our often too-well manicured parks, can support a surprisingly large number of birds. The birds are often most visible where people have congregated to buy, sell, eat, and discard food. City life favors bird species that are less affected by the toxic substances found in our cities, that are able to adapt to artificial light, that can communicate over the noise of traffic, and who can breed successfully on human-built structures.

Birds that are unable to adapt to the human environment disappear and are replaced by the more adaptable birds. Some of the birds that have adapted are surprising, such as the bird-eating Peregrine Falcon. In the wild, it is a cliff-dwelling bird, but it has adapted to nesting on window ledges of high-rise buildings, and finds and an abundant food source in the common pigeon.

The Scarlet Tanager (above), the Lazuli Bunting (opposite), and the Indigo Bunting (page 86) are all only seen in the spring and summer over all of the United States.

Why do some birds appear only seasonally?

No matter where you live, there are several bird species that are present all year round. For many of us, that may be the chickadees or cardinals.

But also, no matter where you live, there are irruptions of birds, birds you might see only for days or weeks, or who might be summer-only or winter-only residents.

Birds that appear for only a few days are those that are stopping by during a long migration. Warblers are one such group, with irruptions of warblers appearing in the fall in many parts of the country as they head south for the winter. The reverse happens in spring.

Some seasonal appearances have to do with birds utilizing a food source. For instance, we've all seen geese fly overhead during the autumn, and yes, they are heading south for the winter.

But they may linger, often for weeks on end, to feed in farm fields on waste grain, far north of where they will eventually spend the winter. Northern

fruit-eating birds, such as the Bohemian Waxwing, will venture as far south as they need to find the dried, clinging fruits of the summer. Unlike true migrations in which birds move from a specific breeding ground to a certain wintering ground, movements like that of the waxwings are much less predictable, and vary depending upon weather.

People who live in the north know that they see some birds only in the summer. The first American Robin of spring, for instance, is a welcome sight. These are birds that nest in your region, but must depart for the winter.

If you live in the south, the reverse often occurs. You will see some birds all winter long, and then some early spring day they will disappear, and you'll know they are returning to their breeding grounds.

The Snowy Owl (opposite) is rarely seen in the lower 48 states, except when the lemming population plunges in the far north. When this happens, Snowy Owls are then seen far from their typical winter ranges, and often, because they are hungry and stressed for food, they are active in daylight.

The Curve-billed Thrasher (above) eats agave flowers and a variety of cactus seeds, including those of Saquaros. The Western Gull (opposite) is an opportunistic omnivore and will eat almost anything, including starfish.

Why do birds eat what they eat?

Songbirds can be divided into two groups: seed (including fruit) eaters and insect eaters. This grouping is imperfect, though, because all birds eat insects at some point in their lives, particularly when young. Insects are rich in protein, which helps young birds grow at a remarkable rate. And of course, there are birds that are not songbirds who are flesh-eating birds, such as eagles and hawks, and birds that graze, such as geese.

All bird species have evolved to utilize nature's numerous niches. Birds have an extremely high metabolism so to keep up with the requirements, they must eat a large amount of food. A small bird can eat up to twenty percent of its body weight daily. It makes sense then that they would focus on abundant foods like seeds and insects. When they come to your feeders, they are merely substituting your offerings for the natural seeds or insects they'd otherwise eat.

You say you don't put out insects for them? No, but if you put out suet,

you are replacing the insect matter that woodpeckers and other birds, like chickadees, would otherwise eat.

In addition to eating a lot of food compared to body weight, birds also need to be efficient foragers. They

need to balance the choice between abundant but perhaps not as nutritious foods, with harder-to-find but more nutritious items. And they may well choose between eating a hard-to-open seed versus one less difficult to crack.

The Greater Roadrunner (opposite left) feeds on large insects, scorpions, lizards, snakes, small rodents, and small birds, including nestlings and hummingbirds. In pursuit of its prey, the bird runs very fast and can outrun many lizards. Turkey Vultures (opposite right), feed almost exclusively on carrion, and small groups will gather at a carcass. The Wood Thrush (right) eats insects, worms, and fruit when available.

The California Quail (above) has legs well developed for walking and running, and is usually seen on the ground in open areas. The running posture of the Greater Roadrunner (opposite) is smooth and strong, allowing it to run down lizards and snakes.

Why do some birds hop, others walk, and some run?

Birds choose their locomotion based on how efficient it is for them, and perhaps also on how it fits their feeding strategy.

Large birds tend to run. Small birds tend to hop. Why is that?

A large bird can run in a similar bipedal mode as you. Doing so allows it to cover ground quickly, whether it is to run down a tasty insect, or escape your neighbor's cat.

But for a small bird, like a Junco, running just doesn't make sense. Its stride would be too short to move very quickly. Yet by hopping, the Junco is able to move at least a full body length in a single motion. Obviously, for it and similar birds, this is far more efficient. You may have seen other ground foragers, such as buntings, towhees, or sparrows, hopping in place amongst leaves and other ground debris. They actually aren't trying to move, but are foraging for food. This technique is called "double scratching," and is practiced by many of the larger sparrows.

Most songbirds hop, but not all. Some, like larks, pipits, starlings, and meadowlarks, typically stride. Not all members of the crow family act the same either; jays hop, crows stride. And some common birds do both – robins and blackbirds either hop or run, depending upon the situation.

Defending his territory, the male Great Egret on the left (above) nips a rival male's leg in the air. Perhaps to drive away the unwanted Double-crested Cormorant (opposite), the Roseate Spoonbill is nipping him on the wing.

Why do birds chase, or fight, with each other?

It isn't at all uncommon to see two birds, often of the same species, tussling with each other near your feeder or in the park. Sometimes they'll even take to the air to continue the battle. What's going on?

When birds of the same species chase each other, one of two things is happening. If they are both males, it is almost certainly a territorial battle. The male in possession of the territory is attempting to drive off the interloper. Since territories can overlap, these conflicts occur most often where they intersect.

If one is a male and the other a female, it could well be an attempt to mate. Females choose the male, and sometimes an overly-energetic male may pursue a female who is not ready to mate. In those cases, she'll rapidly fly away.

Occasionally, birds of different species fight. When this occurs, it is more likely to be in connection with competition for a food source, and sometimes, it just seems birds don't like birds of different species. I've watched birds of one species gladly share food with others of their kind, but peck at a bird of a competing species when it moves in to feed.